Ermias Birhanu Alaro

Formulate the guiding elements and draft the rules that would help to introduce single member companies in Ethiopia

Anchor Academic
Publishing

Birhanu Alaro, Ermias: Formulate the guiding elements and draft the rules that would help to introduce single member companies in Ethiopia, Hamburg, Anchor Academic Publishing 2016

Buch-ISBN: 978-3-95489-449-9
PDF-eBook-ISBN: 978-3-95489-949-4
Druck/Herstellung: Anchor Academic Publishing, Hamburg, 2016

Bibliografische Information der Deutschen Nationalbibliothek:
Die Deutsche Nationalbibliothek verzeichnet diese Publikation in der Deutschen Nationalbibliografie; detaillierte bibliografische Daten sind im Internet über http://dnb.d-nb.de abrufbar.

Bibliographical Information of the German National Library:
The German National Library lists this publication in the German National Bibliography. Detailed bibliographic data can be found at: http://dnb.d-nb.de

All rights reserved. This publication may not be reproduced, stored in a retrieval system or transmitted, in any form or by any means, electronic, mechanical, photocopying, recording or otherwise, without the prior permission of the publishers.

Das Werk einschließlich aller seiner Teile ist urheberrechtlich geschützt. Jede Verwertung außerhalb der Grenzen des Urheberrechtsgesetzes ist ohne Zustimmung des Verlages unzulässig und strafbar. Dies gilt insbesondere für Vervielfältigungen, Übersetzungen, Mikroverfilmungen und die Einspeicherung und Bearbeitung in elektronischen Systemen.

Die Wiedergabe von Gebrauchsnamen, Handelsnamen, Warenbezeichnungen usw. in diesem Werk berechtigt auch ohne besondere Kennzeichnung nicht zu der Annahme, dass solche Namen im Sinne der Warenzeichen- und Markenschutz-Gesetzgebung als frei zu betrachten wären und daher von jedermann benutzt werden dürften.

Die Informationen in diesem Werk wurden mit Sorgfalt erarbeitet. Dennoch können Fehler nicht vollständig ausgeschlossen werden und die Diplomica Verlag GmbH, die Autoren oder Übersetzer übernehmen keine juristische Verantwortung oder irgendeine Haftung für evtl. verbliebene fehlerhafte Angaben und deren Folgen.

Alle Rechte vorbehalten

© Anchor Academic Publishing, Imprint der Diplomica Verlag GmbH
Hermannstal 119k, 22119 Hamburg
http://www.diplomica-verlag.de, Hamburg 2016
Printed in Germany

Acknowledgement

I extend my heartfelt thanks to my Instructor **professor Zekarias Keneaa for** the devotion of time to read, attention for the mini paper; evaluate the presentation, and tremendous help for this course. And also thanks for the reformulation of my title in one Man Company in palatable way and giving the guild line for my work. All the staffs of the Faculty of Law, Jimma University also deserve my thanks for their administrative assistance during my stay and work in Jimma. (Providing internet access in the computer lab)

All my colleagues in Addis Ababa who extended their good wishes to me during the pursuit of the study also deserve my thanks.

My families deserve reward for their patience and encouragement: I love and respect them.

Ermias Birhanu

June, 2013

Abstract

One man company has been admitted by some 36 countries[1] of the world has become an active entity playing important role in the market. In china, the company law revised and promulgated in 2005 stipulate provision for such kind company. However, these new provision are too simple and have some questions unresolved that why the writer predominately prefer the Indian draft bill on one- man company as possible to draft single member company in Ethiopia after taking of other international experiences from Liechtenstein rule, US, EU, UK, Germany, and France.

Therefore, the paper focus on the introduction of one man company law in Ethiopia has factors and basic rule should be known before incorporate one Man Company into Ethiopian legal system. There were suitable conditions as factors to put into Ethiopia legal systems.

There are also the fundamental rules properly regulated before the incorporation of one Man Company in to our legal system after draft the proper regulation on it.

I focus on the palatable content of regulation for Ethiopia as possible draft on single member company from well experienced country by contextualizing it in to our factual situation of Ethiopia.

Basic rule focuses on formation, capital, registration, and regulation at market entry, founder, and operation, and market exit, corporate existence with corporate limited liability, member manager, board of director with social responsibility and creditors' interest.

Finally, the mini paper has a number of recommendations on formation of one Man Company, capital requirement, corporate governances, and director, member manager with personal liability, creditor interest, auditor and high level of inspection.

Key words: One-man Company, limited liability, disregards corporate personality, piercing the corporate veil

---

[1] BERNARD F.CATALDO, LIMITED LIABILITY WITH ONE MAN COMPANY AND SUBSIDIARY CORPORATION 18 LAW AND CONTEMP. PROBS 474(1953).

Table of content

Acknowledgement 5

Abstract 7

1 Introduction /background 11
   1.1 Definition and Nature of One Man Company 12
   1.2 Transferability of one Man Company 13

2 Basic factors for upcoming of one Man Company in general and Basis of legal regime 14
   2.1 Basic factors for upcoming of one man company in Ethiopia 14
   2.2 Legal regime for one Man Company 15
   2.3 The method for regulation of one Man Company 17
      2.3.1 Formation of Single Member Company 17

3 The basic rule for Single member companies and its challenges in Ethiopia 22
   3.1 Basic rule for one Man Company 22
   3.2 Membership requirement in Ethiopia 26
   3.3 Contractual agreement in one Man Company 27

4 Ethiopian legal system and introduction of one Man Company 28
   4.1 International experience on one Man Company 28
   4.2 The possible lesson for Ethiopia to incorporate one man company in to our legal system 38
   4.3 Possible draft of one Man Company 39

5 Recommendation and conclusion 49
   5.1 Conclusion 49
   5.2 Recommendation 50

References 53

1 Introduction /background

Since Liechtenstein, the first country in the world acknowledged the legal position of Single Member Liability Company by statute law, this type of company has been legally recognized in an increasing number of countries.[2] But in practice, England is the first country which paved the way to one man company practice in Solomon case.[3] Since the decision shows the independent corporate existence and limited liability so that the owner of Co. Ltd (Solomon) free from personal liability.

Single Member Company emerged and developed rapidly in recent years, for the reason of their strong economic, political and legal theoretical basis. As a result, we can dig into their emergence and development from a social and historical point of view. It is helpful to encourage investment, develop economy and facilitate employment, and more freedom to the owner of the company. When compared with ordinary types of companies, Single Member Companies' legal characters lie in the singularity of shareholder and the particularity of its corporate governance structure. Thus it increases the possibility for the single shareholder to abuse the rights and damage the interests of companies' creditors and tax authority. In order to protect the company's creditors, it is necessary to regulate single member company strictly and set up integrated creditors protection rules.[4]

Therefore, the legal status for Single Person Companies should be authorized and as well positively standardized in order to seek advantages and avoid disadvantages. Ethiopia has suitable condition when we analysis the factual station a country to introduce and to benefit from the advantage of one man company.

The one man company law as company required to meet requirement on company form (legality), initial capital, qualification and professional integrity for the board of directors, capital adequacy, reserving, fund guarantee (investment for company), accounting, auditing reporting, public disclosure and other corporate governances matters and the like could be vital guiding element for one man company since it is one form of business activities.

---

[2] Beihui Miao, A Comparative Study of Legal Framework for Single Member Company in European Union and China 1 School of Law, King's College London, University of London, London, United Kingdom Correspondence,WC2R 2LS, England, United Kingdom. Tel: 44-788-851-5557.
E-mail:beihui.miao@kcl.ac.uk at 1
[3] Solomon & co.(1889),[1897]A.C (H.L) in saloman v. saloman & co. case and also see infra note 5.
[4] Supra note 1

1.1 Definition and Nature of One Man Company

What is One Person Company? Company formed by a single person, One-person Company in the legal system is a move that would encourage corporatization of business and OPC is a one entrepreneurship legal and financial liability is limited shareholder corporate entity to the company only.[5]

One-man companies are the companies in which one man holds virtually the whole of the share capital with a few extra members holding the remainder, who may be his relations or nominees in single member Company. Being the largest holder such a person is generally the sole or the managing director and enjoys complete control over the single member company. This is done with a view to fulfill the statutory requirement of at least five members in the case of a public company/share company and at least two members in the case of a private company (PLC). He is, thus, in a position to enjoy the profits of the business with limited corporate liability. Such types of companies are perfectly valid and not illegal. As already established in saloman v. saloman & co. ltd case, such companies are legal entities distinct from the members that why the single member (Solomon) shall not be personal liable.[6]

Limited liability: - limited liability of single member is one of the most common characteristics of one man Company. One man company is a separate legal entity. It is the owner of its assets and liable to pay its liability. In other words liability of the single member is limited. A single member is liable to contribute anything not more than the nominal value of the company held by him.[7] If the asset of the company is insufficient to meet the claims of the creditors of the one man company, the single member cannot be asked to pay anything more than what is due on the capital of the one man company by him.

The privilege of limited liability for business debts is one of the important advantages of doing business under one man Company since the liability will not extend to the private property of the single member, unlike that of sole partnership.

---

[5] Bizand Legis, OPC one person company, available at http://www.bizandlegis.com (date of assessed June 21, 2013) and also see Section 2(62) One Person Company (OPC) Bill in India(2012), available at http://www.mca.gov.in/Ministry/pdf/The_Companies_Bill_2012.pdf

[6] Beihui Miao, A Comparative Study of Legal Framework for Single Member Company in European Union and China Journal of Politics and Law; Vol. 5, No. 3; 2012, ISSN 1913-9047 E-ISSN 1913-9055, Published by Canadian Center of Science and Education at1 and also see infra not 43.

[7] The derivative of commercial cod of Ethiopia 1960's, share company provisions applies to single member company in way of "mutatis mutandis" in the area gab (nature ,form, capacity , legal personality , owner of company, outsider ,BOD, creditors, manager, capital, founder(s),MA, AA, Registration, commercial gazette, bankruptcy and wind- up) the writer of this mini paper take principle form share company to single member company with modification since it need some kind of contextualizing the provisions into one man company.

Perpetual succession: - unlike partnership one man company will not be dissolved by the death or incapacity of its single member of one Man Company. It is an entity with a perpetual succession. Its life is not measured by the life of a single member. It is independent of the lives of its single member. He may come and may go, but the company continues its operation unless it is wound-up.[8]

1.2 Transferability of one Man Company

Even though it is possible to restrict free transfer of one Man Company in the articles of association. As a general principle a company is freely transferable and can be sold or purchased in the market. This is one of the reasons why people prefer to form single member companies than partnerships. Transferability of a man company is an added advantage both to the institution of the one man company as well as to the investor interims profit. The company's capital becomes a permanent and stable feature of the company because the owner cannot with draw anything out of it.[9] Hence, it is vital to protect the interest of creditor.

---

[8] Ibid
[9] Ibid

2 Basic factors for upcoming of one Man Company in general and Basis of legal regime

2.1 Basic factors for upcoming of one man company in Ethiopia

The factual situation of the country palatable/suitable condition for introduction one man company[10] since the people want to work alone in small business because the people has individualistic mentality (i.e. kewisk mentality or jabelo mentality) since the desire of the people in business is individualistic in nature not collective stand in mega corporation. This is because of the fear of being cheat and also the business people need limited liability (they fear risk).

Therefore, individualistic nature of Ethiopian people can be ground for introduction of one Man Company because the introduction has advantage of corporate existences and limited corporate liability.[11]

Many entrepreneurs are "refugees" from the large corporate world (not common in Ethiopia), while others choose to be self-employed in a "one-person company" as a change from a traditional-based small business with employees and increased management responsibilities. Being unemployed after another wave of outsourcing to Ethiopia can also trigger the desire in people to become self-employed and especially to stay a "one-person company" if the law allows single member company in Ethiopia. Especially the political games played in larger corporations increase the desire to completely get away from the same. Being flexible and able to implement decisions without having to worry about the "internal political players" is a driving force to work alone. our people does not want to engage in company politics in addition to fear of loss on their investment that why the prefer sole proprietorships (which is heights in number since people does not want to invest their money to gather in huge corporation rather they prefer sole entrepreneurship or small business alone)[12]

---

[10] One man company principle equally applies for one woman company in the whole mini paper that I use single member company or man company or one person company(OPC) interchangeable

[11] Professor Zekarias kenaa,(lecture), individualistic nature of people of Ethiopia in small business(jeblo mentality) could be factor introduction of single member company , Jimma university ,Jimma, date of presentation at may 22-2013 ff. (e- mail zenkente@yahoo.com)

[12] Data from Ethiopia investment agency and from trade and industry offices

2.2 Legal regime for one Man Company

The FDRE constitution provided that "every Ethiopian has the right to engage freely in economic activity and to pursue a livelihood..."[13] at basis of this article the economic activities in include all forms of business activities; hence, one man company is one form of business activities. Due to this, an individual has constitutional base to engage freely in one Man Company to pursue a livelihood and 'an individual has right to ownership of the private property'[14] in the form of business activities like by establishing one man company since it is one form of private ownership of property. Therefore, the FDRE constitution allows the formation of one man company since it is one form of economic activities or business activities. But, there is no recognition of one Man Company in the commercial cod of Ethiopia.

However, Article 510 of the Draft stipulates that there can be a single-member private limited company. But no additional rules are provided as to how the concept can be integrated in this part of the Code. Based on a study on the ramifications and implications of introducing such a company, additional rules need to be incorporated[15]

So, same may wonder why anyone would choose to register as a sole proprietary company rather than as a single proprietorship. Well, there are some real advantages to being registered as a sole shareholder/director company. Some of the reasons people choose one man company over a proprietorship are:

Legal personality of company:-Once a company is registered with the ASIC and a CAN (commercial registrar in Ethiopia) has been is issued, the company becomes a legal entity with a personality that is independent and separate from its shareholder.

This distinct personality has important legal effects: A single member company can enter into contracts in its own name and it can also sue, and be sued. When a one man company is in debt, the money owed does not automatically become the debt of the shareholder. As a result, a civil lawsuit for the collection of a sum of money against the company is not necessarily a legal action against the shareholder (owner).

---

[13] FEDERAL DEMOCRATIC REPABLIC OF ETHIOPIA CONSTITUTION OF 1995 , ARTICLE 41(1)
[14] Id at article 40(1)
[15] RECOMMENDATIONS AND POSITION PAPER OF THE BUSINESS COMMUNITY ON THE REVIS OF THE COMMERCIAL CODE OF ETHIOPIA Prepared by A TEAM OF FOURTEEN NATIONAL EXPER34 (july2008)

This is because the liability of a shareholder is limited to the value of his shareholdings unless he previously signed a personal guarantee in favor of the one pursuing legal action. This built-in limitation is not available in single proprietorships or for sole traders. So if he is conducting business by himself, and he wish to limit his business liability, then the sole shareholder proprietary company is for him.

Flexibility in ownership:-If his business grows in the future and he wishes to create incentives for his non-shareholder employees who have contributed to the success of his company, then a good way is to increase their involvement by transferring shares in the company to them.

This is also known as a stock option. Because of the company's structure, he is able to accommodate additional non-shareholder employees into the company shareholdings without having to terminate the company's legal status.[16] This principle could be in line with FDRE constitution article 40(1) "freedom on private ownership" and article 41(1) freedom in the choice of form business activities.[17]

Continuity:-Another advantage of the independent personality of the company is that it may continue to exist for the duration of its registration, notwithstanding changes in the ownership of the company's shares.

The death or retirement of a shareholder or the sale, transfer or assignment of the rights to a company's shares will not mean the termination of a company's existence. he may one day decide to hand over the reins of the company to someone else, such as one of his experienced managers or employee-shareholders. While the director may be changed, the company continues to exist as its registered self.[18]

It is possible to register a company online, but if this is a daunting prospect for him, ASIC has appointed registered agents, like Companies now who can advise and manage his online company registration.[19]Therefore, the nature and the advantage of one Man Company could be deferent from other form business activities like partnership, Share Company and PLCs.

---

[16] Can One Person form a Company? Available at www.companiesnow.com.au, date of accessed may 30-2013
[17] Federal democratic republic of Ethiopia (FDRE) constitution in 1995
[18] Ibid
[19] I bid

2.3 The method for regulation of one Man Company

2.3.1 Formation of Single Member Company

A company may have a single member by virtue of its being formed, or by virtue of all its shares coming to be held by a single person (natural or artificial person). In other words, a company may have a sole member when it is formed and also when all its shares come to be held by a single person. To the extent that a single person or single member, states choose to recognize the concept, Single Member Companies/one Man Company may be created both *ab initio* and on a subsequent concentration of all shares with only one owner, in the single member company directive if we draft that.[20]

Despite the title of the Directive, it will apply not only where the sole owner of the company is a natural person but also where the owner is a legal person. Thus the Directive will also be relevant in group relationships with 100% owned subsidiaries. So far, the Directive presents no bar to the states maintaining special rules in cases in which a natural person is the single company participant in several companies or a legal person is the only participant in a company.[21]

In an earlier draft the Commission wanted to go as far as imposing a ban against one legal person being sole owner of another company. These proposals which appeared very formalistic and which undoubtedly would be easy to circumvent have been renounced. Thereby the single-member Company Directive provisions could be focused on their central purpose: to facilitate the access of liability limitation for small and medium size business with one single owner.[22] Therefore, these formation stage requirements should be incorporated into Ethiopian legal systems on the future draft law of one Man Company.

Under the Old Company Law share company, PLCs, a limited liability company was required to have two or more shareholders. The New Company Law or one Man Company now allows natural persons or legal persons to form single shareholder limited liability companies. The new statute provides for a simplified management structure appropriate to single shareholder entities. However, in order to prevent abuse of the corporate structure in single shareholder companies, the one man company provides for a number of restrictions:[23]

---

[20] Beihui Miao ,A Comparative Study of Legal Framework for Single Member Company in European Union and China at page 7
[21] .ibid
[22] Ibid
[23] Steven M. Dickinson ,Harris & Moure, Introduction to the New Company Law of the People's Republic of China, at 3

17

- The registered minimum capital requirement should be 250,000 EB at base of current reality of Ethiopia.
- The entire registered capital must be paid in a single installment since fully paid at time
- A single investor may form only one single shareholder company, no more than this.
- if the shareholder fails to maintain separation between the financial affairs of the company and the shareholder's personal finances, the shareholder will lose the protection of limited liability and will have joint financial liability for company debts. Therefore, these could be relevant rule to draft one man company in Ethiopia.

A .Minimum capital

Fix the amount of capital in every company is vital including the one man company. What is a need of fixing minimum capital for one Man Company? This for the purpose of protecting the public interest in general (like interims of business taxation and for the statically evidence of the company) and third party interest specifically the creditor interest.

Minimum capital requirement:-now day the value of the birr devaluated because of inflation in the economy that why I recommend that the minimum capital requirement for one man company at least 250,000 birr and also the minimum capital for the PLCs could be the 250,000 birr[24] in future .these is because PLCs in effect become part of defacto one man company in Ethiopia. Since PLCs usually establish among one family (child, wife are the member of PLC) but in effect one person is the owner of the capital of PLCs and the profit therein that why writer considered the PLCs as defacto one man company in Ethiopia since in effect there are many single member PLCs.

B .Deposit and Registration

The following documents must be deposited at the office of registrar that is Ministry of Trade and Industry at Federal level and Trade and Industry Bureau's at regional level.

1. The memorandum of association
2. The articles of association
3. all complementary documents before and during formation of one man company

---

[24] NB 1$=1EB in 1960's (HSI regime), but now 1$=17EB, therefore, 15,000 x 17 =255,000EB that why the writer recommend approximately, the fixed capital should be 250,000 birr. This amount of capital applies for PLCs=single member private company=defacto one man company =formal one man company in near future.

These documents are accompanied by an application demanding the registration of the company in the books of commercial register. The registration is of capital importance, for the company does not require legal personality until it has been entered in the registry of commercial registration. So, one man company acquires legal personality as soon as it is entered in the registry of commercial registration. [25]This means that it is there up on it acquires the legal capacity (let assume as draft law of one man company would consists) as it will provide by Law. These will include:-

- a name of one man company specified in its statutes
- a registered office, which is the main address where the management of the one man company is located. This registered office must be specified in the statutes.
- The power to do acts with legal effect:- In that it may acquire property and may acquire or become subject to rights and liabilities. The assets of the one man company are therefore separate from the assets of its single member (owner), and the latter have rights in the one man company but not directly in its assets. Because the asset belongs to one man company as independent legal entity.
- The power to sue and to defend legal proceedings against it. These are because of corporate existence and limited liability of one Man Company.[26]

Amendment

A company has a statuary right to amend its memorandum and articles of association by single member through notification of creditors, ministry trade and industry.

Securities

One man Company can issue debt of securities but if single member wants to change from single member in to share company it is possible to issues the equity security to increase the capital of the new formed company without affecting the interest of third parties and federal the tax authority.[27]Hence, he has duty to give notification to concerned authority like tax authority, ministry of trade and industry, registrar office of the country.

---

[25] BERNARD F.CATALDO,LIMITED LIABILITY WITH ONE MAN COMPANIES AND SUBSIDIARY CORPORTION:18 LAW AND CONTEPT PROBS 474(1953)
[26] Mario Rotondi, limited liability of the individual trade: one –man company or commercial foundation:48 TULL.L.Rev.474,(1973-1974)
[27] Ibid

Debt securities in one man company :- holders of debt securities are creditors and rank prior to unsecured creditors, debt securities are remunerated by fixed interest ,only bond issues may be secured by issuer(one man company) and debt securities are issued for a defined term and are reimbursed to their holders.

C .Founder

Before one man company can be formed, there must be some person(s) who have an intention to form a single member company and who take the necessary steps to carry that intention into operation. Such person(s) are called founders. The word 'founder' has not been defined any where in the commercial code. Founder may be the owner of one Man Company or out side of the ownership of one Man Company. [28]

However, the founder is a person who brings one man company into existence. He/she is one who undertakes to form one man company with reference to a given object and to set it going and who takes the necessary steps to accomplish that purpose. The founder(s) decide the scope and business of one Man Company. He/They prepare the necessary documents. He/They make arrangements for advertising/notification to the concerned regulatory and to public.[29]

One man Company may have single/one or several/more founder(s). A founder may be an individual or body corporate. One existing body corporate may be founder of new one Man Company. A person who is not member of the newly formed one man company, but acts in a professional activity, (such persons being solicitor, engineer, accountant or valuer) for the founding of the one man company are also founder(s) of the single member company. Founder(s) is/are the following: [30]

- Founder(s) is/are persons who sign the memorandum of association and paid the whole of the capital or.
- Any person outside of the company who initiated the plans of facility the formation of the one man company

---

[28] Mario Rotondi , Supra note 25 at 474ff.
[29] Supra note 7, art 307 comm.cod ff
[30] Id

Roles, Rights and Liabilities of Founder

Roles: - founder(s) are not agents because there is no principal because single member company is under formation. However, founders from the moment they start to act with the name of the company they stand in a fiduciary position towards the one man company under formation. They have the power of creating and modifying the single member company. They may enter into commitments/contracts with third parties in the name of the one man company, but they may be refunded after the company has taken over this commitments and the one man company may only take over if the commitments taken by the founder(s) were necessary for the formation of the one man company. But, usually the founder could be the owner or become single member of the one man company.

Rights:-The nature of the founder(s) work in the formation of the one man company call for the considerable skill for which he should be paid sum amount of money which shall not exceed one tenth of the net profits in the balance sheet. Such amount must be stated in memorandum of association. In the absence of such statement, a founder has no right against the company for his payment.[31] If it is stated it is presumed that there is a contract which gives the directors power to pay the preliminary expenses out of the company's funds. Such benefit may not extend for more than two years and the founder(s) have no any other right than the one stated in this paragraph.

Liabilities: - concerning liabilities of the founder(s), the violation of those acts may lead into the violation of stated provision and this in turn may result into criminal liability and criminal liability is borne by the doer personally not to be transferred to third party. If the required capital (250,000 birr) and which is not fully paid then it is violation of law; for example, the minimum capital required to form one man Company with less than stated amount (250,000 birr). Similarly, the capital of one Man Company should be fully paid up at formation stage. If founders formed one man company without fully paid, such will lead to the violation of the law.[32] As to the contribution in kind, it must be full paid, it must be done by an expert, and be verified at least three times (founder, auditors, and ministry trade and industry).[33] If the amount does not conform to exact value then there is violation of the law by the founder(s) this is because of the interest of third parties like creditors', public, government from misleading the capital of one man company when there were over evolution(misled creditors) or undervaluation(misled tax authority)

---

[31] Supra note 7 at art.308 com cod ff
[32] BERNARD F.CATALDO, Supra note 22 at 475ff.
[33] Supra note 7 at art. 309 comm. cod

3 The basic rule for Single member companies and its challenges in Ethiopia

The formation stages of one Man Company include legal form, ownership, and minimum capital. Moreover, not only the name of the one Man Company "under formation" could be one of basic rule but also tenure of auditors, director(s), manger(s) with inspiration and examination. These and the like corporate governance, corporate existences, registration, corporate limited liability, single member right and power of decision with third party interest could be the basis for rule of one Man Company.

One man company as company has profit goal, separate ownership, single member, and corporate governance (transparency, registration, manager, auditor, BODs) introduced clearing and settlement system to protect government and the interest third parties usually creditors.

3.1 Basic rule for one Man Company

1) Strict capital ascertainment principle should be carried out. The registered capital of single member company must be no less than two hundred fifty thousand (250,000) EB and must be paid up at one time; or fully subscribed and full paid up at time of incorporation and a least two time inspection is important for one man company to avoid abuse therein.

2) Rule on contribution in kind shall be fully paid at time of formation of the company[34] and may not be delayed beyond the date of registration of the one man company. With this respect to this provision of share company shall apply for one Man Company through "mutatis mutandis"

3) The single member company must be clearly written on its business license that it is exclusively invested by solo natural person or solo legal person;

4) One natural person is allowed to have only one Single Person Company which means it is prohibited to set up another Company for one physical person; but it possible to him to set up share company, PLCs, other business activities.[35] Since if a single individual has more than one Man Company, then it will open the door for fraud and abuse on business taxation and creditor interests. Hence, these limitations up on the owner of one Man Company should be

---

[34] Commercial cod article 339(1) and see supra note 3.
[35] YANG BEIJING, WANG YONG, Infra note 50

for the sack of creditors' interest and the public interest. But these limitation does not apply for the juridical persons because they have right to establish more than one man company i.e. one artificial person shall have more than one single member company.[36]

5) One Person Company should prepare financial report every fiscal year and have it audited by an officially approved accounting firm;

6) In the event of liability dispute, the shareholder of the single member company has the responsibility to prove that his properties are separate from the company's assets. If not the shareholder loses the rights that he is limited to his invested property for the liabilities and he has to take unlimited responsibilities for company's debt occurred.[37] Therefore, Rule must makes distinction between personal propriety and one man company assets.

7) Rule also made that there must be independent registration, publicity, notification to regulator, to public at the same time because of its unique nature.[38] Unless it misled creditors, open door for abuse, it affects the interest of government interims of business taxation.

8).Rule made that there must have good corporate governance (interims of transparency, registration and publicity or information, auditor(s), managements, modernizing board of directors and manager, and single shareholder right and his democracy like freedom of decision in his company) in consideration of all stock holders

9) The fundamental minimum requirement of one man company (a)capital fully subscribed and full paid by single member at least in principle(b)vital administrative set (c) evaluation of contribution in kind at least three time founder(he himself or out sider),auditor, and ministry trade and industry.

10) set maximum age limit on board member of one man company unless they are not position disclose the information for government (public),third party(like creditor) these because to protect the abuse act of the company or the owner of the company. The executives and manager of one Man Company does not have contractual agreement or claim, additional benefit from single member (owner) of the company

11) Rule on merger of one Man Company with share company, PLCs is allowed in principle but merger of one Man Company with other one man company allows as an exceptional

---

[36] Pinsent Masons, Introduction to China's New Company Law February 2006 available at, www.pinsentmasons.com
[37] Steven M. Dickinson ,Harris & Moure ,Supra note 22 at 9
[38] Ibid

circumstances like one of single member company become weak in management and profit making with court authorization by the claim of interested party.

12) Rule on conversation of one Man Company into Share Company. (a) by the operation of the law (b) by choice of the owner[39] in both cases the interest government (interims business taxation) and interest of third party like creditors should be protected by law. Whereas merger in one Man Company with Share Company, PLCs, and other one man company in that case, the protection is not only government (public interest) and creditor interest, but also consumer protection from unfair competition and abuse of market.

13) Conversation by default shall not apply for one Man Company.[40]

14) Limitation up on the owner of a company from equity investment participation when there is the possibility of abuse/fraud done by him. So, any interested parties apply to the concerned authority/ court if there is possibility of abusive acts of the owner the company.

15) One man company cannot engage in insurance, banking, MFI or other similar business.[41]

16) One man company is a company whose capital is fixed in advance and whose liability are met only by the assets of the single member company. The single member company shall be liable only to the extent of his capital in the company, hence, liability of the company up to the extent of its assets because the independent corporate existences.

17) the owner shall not be personal liable when he has not acted as managers and even if he has been manager of his own company so long as he prove that he has acted with due care and due diligence then he is not personal liable even if the asset of his company was not adequate to cover the claim of the creditor(s).[42]

18) the liability of directors when the assets of the company are found to be inadequate to settle the claims of third party creditors where they fail to preserve intact the one man company's assets.[43]

---

[39] AVTAR SINGH, COMPANY LAW, FOURTEENTH EDITION, 533FF(2004)
[40] Supra note 35 and also see Id at 534.
[41] Company in financial institution in the form of share company only, so that bank, insurances proclamation no 592/2008 and 746/2012 respectively allows only bank share company, insurances share company. Even number of restriction the amount of share in bank and insurances by one family sine the law prohibit them from having share company among one family So that let alone one person even a few persons or one family can not establish bank, insurances this to protect the financial institution from market dominances and abuse
[42] Which derived from the commercial cod of Ethiopia article 531(2) and china new law / one man company law (2005)
[43] Ibid

19) The single member shall not be the creditor of his own one man company and also he shall not claim a right as creditor in the time of winding –up (liquidation) the one man company.

20) the single member company shall have chair man of board of directors (usually the owner of the company) and other member of board of director(s) from out sider (those does not have share in one man company) for the sack of social responsibility in order to protect the environmental and human right issues[44]

21) Rule keep that on record, that who will inherit or control the one man company if that first person dies / or incapacitated.[45]

> "Provided that the memorandum of One Person Company shall indicate the name of the other person, with his prior written consent in the prescribed form, who shall, in the event of the subscriber's death or his incapacity to contract become the member of the company and written consent of such person shall also be filed with the Registrar at the time of incorporation of the One Person Company along with its memorandum and articles:"[46]

Therefore, the death/ incapacitation of owner of the company do not affect the legal personality of one man company and creditor interest.

22) Rule, the person has to nominate a name with that person's written consent as a nominee to the OPC. This person will be the default and ad hoc member in case of the existing sole member's death or disability. This provision will ensure perpetuity and continuity to the life of the Company. The golden rule of "single member may come and go, but the Company must live on" holds good.

23) Rule the person is to give a separate name and legal identity to the Company, under which all the activities of the business are to be carried on.

24) Finally, every One Person Company should bear the letters "OPC" or one man company in brackets after its registered name, wherever it may be printed, affixed or engraved.

---

[44] King report of the executive summary, king committee on corporate governance,11,IOD,INSTITUTE OF DIRECTORS,(march 2002)
[45] Faridabad Small Industries Association The face of Modern Indian MSMEs www.fsiaindia.com FSIA Park , Opp. Plot No.23, Sector-24, Faridabad- 121005, Haryana , India & Integrated Association of Micro, Small & Medium Enterprises of India www.iamsmeofindia.co.in E-mail: fsiaindia@gmail.com, info@iamsmeofindia.co.in +91-9711123111 (Executive Secretary)
[46] Section 3(1)(c) One Person Company (OPC) Bill in India(2012), available at http://www.mca.gov.in/Ministry/pdf/The_Companies_Bill_2012.pdf

25) Rule, One man can form a one man company by subscribing their names or his name to a memorandum and complying with the requirements of this possible draft in respect of registration:

- Provided that the memorandum of One Person Company shall indicate the name of the other person also, with his prior written consent in the prescribed form, who shall, in the event of the owner's death become the member of the company and the written consent of such person shall also be filed with the Registrar at the time of incorporation of the One Person Company along with its memorandum and articles
- Provided further that such other person may withdraw his consent in such manner as may be prescribed in the future draft law.
- Provided also that the member of One Person Company may at any time change the name of such other person by giving notice in such manner as may be prescribed.
- Provided also that it shall be the duty of the member of One Person Company to intimate the company the change, if any, in the name of the other person nominated by him by indicating in the memorandum or otherwise within such time and in such manner as may be prescribed, and the company shall intimate the Registrar any such change within such time and in such manner as may be prescribed.
- Provided also that any such change in the name of the person shall not be deemed to be an alteration of the memorandum.

3.2 Membership requirement in Ethiopia

The membership requirement in one Man Company is one of the mandatory requirements and it has the serious consequences for non fulfillment of the membership requirement. so that only one person is requirement for the membership of one man company and also the same person cannot be a member of other single member company. Therefore, there is no nominee member under single member company since it prohibit subordinate member within one Man Company. These could be the possible rule with respect to membership requirement to draft one man company in Ethiopia.

3.3 Contractual agreement in one Man Company

One man company affect the requirement of the contractual agreement as per article 211 commercial cod of Ethiopia[47] since only single member in one man company that why it is not easy to "it take two to tango" that means "it take two to contract" since the agreements where by two or more person. Hence, one man company face difficult to meet the contractual agreement as per commercial cod since only one person in a company unlike partners in partnerships.

However, owner is the agent of one Man Company due this "contract with one self" as his own capacity since he is owner of the company and as a representative capacity(he is an agent to company from the pre-establishment up to end of one man company). Therefore, there is contractual agreement with one self in two capacities agent (owner of the one man company i.e. his own capacity and as agent of the company) as per article 2187cc so that it does not refuit or affects "it takes two to contract"[48] as per the civil code of Ethiopia.

Moreover, the owner of one Man Company could be natural person, juridical person and also the company itself has independent corporate existences as legal person so that these two persons have contractual agreement in this form of business activity. But, our commercial cod does not recognize the one man company so that it needs future looking forward.

---

[47] Commercial cod of Ethiopia in 1960's (article 211comm.cod),and civil cod of Ethiopia article 1675cc,2188,2189 civil cod of Ethiopia.
[48] Civil cod of Ethiopia in 1960's (article 2187 and article 2188cc) and also the lecture note of professor Zekarias kenaa, date of presentation may 21 -2013, e-mail zekentes@yahoo.com.

4 Ethiopian legal system and introduction of one Man Company

In Ethiopian legal system, there is no legal basis for one man company at current time but in practice single member private limited company exist in Ethiopia without appointment of auditor, manager and without making the clear distinction between the full power of manager within the objective of the company and the function of the meeting (owner(s)) that why is the most problematic company in Ethiopian legal system and it become the defacto one man company in Ethiopia. So that PLCs become single member companies in Ethiopia when we analysis the factual condition of a country from the practical point of view. Therefore, formal introduction of one Man Company resolves the legal and practical problems of private limited company.

Moreover, accession of WTO, the influences of globalization, factual situation of Ethiopia can be palatable condition or ground for the introduction of one Man Company.

With respect to accession to WTO aground for liberalization and equal treatment every form business activities including one man company because it is one form of business/economic activities. Therefore, after accession foreign investor can establish the one man company. In the same fashion, globalization forces our door to be opened for one Man Company. So, we should being ready for that force by preparing effective regulation to govern the one man company by taken into account of international experience on one man company. (See below)

Therefore, our introduction to the relevant provision will focus on the following aspects which kind of one man-company was permitted, the disclosure requirement, the capital requirement, other restriction of establishment of one man company and rule of disregarding corporate personality (whether accepting such rule and condition for implementation) or other measure to protect the creditors interests and tax authority interest.

4.1 International experience on one Man Company

A .Liechtenstein rule

As first country in the world to prescribe for one man limited liability Company and joint – stock company the provision are comprehensive and detailed rules as reflected in article 637 to 648 of the 1925 related natural person and one Man Company.

1) Type: one person or legal entity can incorporate any legal entity stipulated in the code (including joint –stock company ,limited liability company)entity reduces only one ,the legal

entity continue to exist, provided that this does not conflict with provision in the company article of association[49]

2) Article of association and disclosure: the article of association of one Man Company shall be in the form of notarial deed. These article associations shall at least contain the following contents.

- A) Name, sit and purpose of the single member company
- B))total amount of capital ,the amount of capital already fully paid in, the amount of half of the minimum capital requirement, total amount of the share issued, whether the shareholder is absolutely limited liability or has the obligation to further contribution capital(contribution in kind could be one form of capital contribution)
- C) Whether the shareholder will be the business executor of the company; if not, how will the management board be organized, especially the business execution organ and the representative organ within the company.
- D) The form of the intent expressions when the company such intent to third party[50]

3) Liability of sole shareholder: the shareholder will be personally liable for the following damage

- A) Suffered by the creditor of the legal entity in the transaction as such: the sole shareholder acts as the representative of the one man company and another legal entity simultaneously during the transaction and such damage is cause because of the shareholder's gross negligence in his representative actions.
- B) Suffered by the one man company because of the negligence of the sole shareholder acting as the business executor or representative.
- C) Suffered by creditor of the one man company because of the gross negligence of the sole shareholder acting as the business executor or representative[51]

4) Dissolution and liquidation of one Man Company: when the debt of the company has reached of the company property or above, under the following circumstances, the creditor can apply to the court to dissolution and liquidation of the company after drawing caution money.

- A) The sole holder acts the business executor of the company, and the creditor suffered significant damage because of his improper action in the management of the company.

---

[49] Item 638, law related to natural person and company(Gesetzuber das personon und Gesellschaftsererchr)
[50] Item 638, law related to natural person and company ((Gesetzuber das personon und Gesellschaftsererchr)
[51] Item 641, law related to natural person and company ((Gesetzuber das personon und Gesellschaftsererchr)

B) The sole shareholder intentionally violation is proved the damage caused by such violation. In both case sole shareholder shall be personally liable beyond the asset of his company.

B. European Union

European Union (EU) is a union by Europe countries to fight against America International Corporation after the Second World War.[52] EU developed from the European communities (EU).because there are many differences among the member states' economic and trade legal systems, which had resulted in many obstacles to the member states' mutual trade, EU made many legal directives to guide the member states to revise their own company laws. In all, EU issued thirteen directives. Although these directives have no binding force on the member states, the member states have the obligation to revise their company law according to these directives.

Among these directives, the twelfth council company law directive on single-member private limited –liability companies was issued on 21 December 1989. The regulations about one Man Company in member state were different from each other before this directive coming forth, and the EU has consistently been promoting the development of middle-small enterprises, especially individual enterprises. These two reasons commonly promoted the twelfth directive.[53] The main content of the directive are as follows

1) Type: a company may have a sole member when it is formed and also when all its shares come to share held by a single person (single-member Company)[54]

2) Disclosure: the disclosure requirements are as follows

　A) When the entire shares have been held by a single shareholder, the identity of the single member must be disclosed by entry in a register accessible to the public;

　B) When decisions are taken by the sole member in his capacity as general meeting, they must be recorded in mints or drawn up in writing;

　C) When contract between a sole member and his company as represented by him are concluded, such contract must be recorded in minutes or drawn up in writing, insofar as such contracts do not relate to current operations concluded under normal conditions[55]

---

[52] Hong Deqin ,European Union: Theory And Policy, Graduate School Of Europe And The United States Of Central Academe At 4. German Stock Act ,China Political And Law University ,2002
[53] Zhao Deshu, Detailed Analysis To One Man Company, China Renmin University Press ,28 (2004) And Also See Twelfth Council Company Law Directive.
[54] Twelfth Council Company Law Directive, Article 2

3) 0ther restriction

- A) Member states may lay down certain special provisions or penalties for cases where a natural person is the sole member of several companies or where a single –member company or any other legal person is the sole member of a company ;
- B) Member states may in specific cases lay down restrictions on the use of single- member companies or remove the limits on the liabilities of sole members;
- C) Member states are free to lay down rules to cover the risks that single- member companies may represent as a consequence of having single members, particularly to ensure that the subscribed capital paid[56]

C. United state

State legislation: in the united states, all states haves their own legislative power and the state courts can establishment their own rule concerning specific issue, therefore the development of rule for one man company different state were not the same. More and more states recognize the legal status of the one man company, until 1980, there are 28 states recognize the legality of one man company.[57]

General speaking, the present status of rule on one –man company in the United States is as follows

1) Types: one man company can be incorporated. It can be inferred that the transferred one man company is also permitted because there should be less obstacle for this than newly established one.

2) Capital: there is no clear requirement for minimum capital of one Man Company. It is commonly admitted that the capital of the company should 'meet the expectable strains of a business of its size and nature". This is a flexible standard.[58] And whether the capital is adequate should be decided case by case[59] but in principle fixing the capital in advances is

---

[55] Twelfth Council Company Law Directive, Article 2
[55] Twelfth Council Company Law Directive, Article 3-5
[56] Twelfth Council Company Law Directive, Introduction
[57] Jan Yuan Ju Zhi, One Man Company, Dongbei University, Jurisprudence, Volume 37 ,No 1 ,39 (1973),Cited From Zhao Deshu , Detail Analysis To One Man Company, China Renmin University Press,39(2004)
[58] "In A Number Of Instances Liability Has Been Imposed Up On A Parent Corporation For The Debts Of Its Subsidiary Where The Capital Of The Later Was Grossly Inadequate For The Normal Strains Of The Business." Warner Fuller ,The Incorporated Individual: A Study Of One Man Company,30
[59] Arnold V Phillips,313 U.S.583;61 S.Ct. 1102,(1941).In Which An Entrepreneur Who Wanted To Operate A Brewery Invested Authored Share Capital $50,000in Cash And Another 75,000 As The Loan To The Corporation For Its Operation, Upon The Insolvency Of The Corporation, It 75,000was Treated As A Capital

vital for the government (to assess the total GDP, to fix the business tax on the company and for the creditor as well) Unless 'flexible standard' open the door the abusive action of owner of company. Therefore, fixing capital, in one Man Company, in country like Ethiopia could be highly recommendable unless it was subject to fraud and abusive acts of the owner.

3) Disregard corporate personality: the rule of disregarding corporate personality is well developed in state united state and as to the condition to disregard corporate personality; the standard now is very detailed. The rule was first mention in bank of the United States v Deveaux (1809) as a dictum. From the late 19th century, the rule has been developing rapidly to from the conditions for the application of the rule. The development can be divided in to three stages[60]

A) The 1st stage (late 19th century to 1910): the applicable situations where: the debtor made use of the corporation to be a barrier, so that he can shift off the debt, escape from the contract liabilities, escape from the liability for his breach of duty.61And the main purpose in this stage is to protect the creator from damages caused by fraud or escaping from obligation etc

B) The 2nd stage (1910-around 1939): the basis for disregarding corporate personality was whether they exists "inequitable" consequence. This standard developed into "complete control or domination" –us marized by Powell in his parent and subsidiary corporation liability of a parent corporation for their obligation of its subsidiary (1931) as "instrumentality theory". One factor is to check whether there corporate personality is independent after the incorporation. If the company is only an instrument if the investor, then the corporate personality should be disregarded62 the main purpose in this stage is to avoid the minority shareholders and the creditors suffered because of the combination of the enterprises group.

C) The 3rd stage (after1939): the standards are the more flexible "justice", "equitable" and the principle has controlling shareholders owns fiduciary duty to creditors while these standards are more effective. As to the principle –subsidiary company,"deep rock doctrine" was set up in 1939 to deal with the provider of the principle company's loan to

---

Contribution. Bernard F. Cataldo, Limited Liability With One Man Companies And Subsidiary Corporation,18 Aw &Contemp.Probs.474,484-485(1953)

[60] The Development Of The Rule In The United States Is Referring To Relative Part Of Zhao Deshu, Detail Analysis To One Man Company, China Renmin University Press,39(2004).

[61] People V The Northern River Sugar Refining Co ; State V Standard Oil Co. Moore & Handle Hardware Co. V Towers Hardware Co. ;Hahine V California Petroleum & Asphalt Co.

[62] Berry Vs Old South Engraving Co.(1993)34

the subsidiary. For any companies have principle –subsidiary. For any companies have principle- subside relationships, if the subsidiary company's capital was not adequate to meet the expectable strains of business of its size and nature, and its operation is controlled by the principle one man company, and the operation is not running normally, then the loan of the principal company to the subsidiary company should subordinated to other creditors, regardless of the character of the loan63

D) and for the one –man company ,it is settled that if the business or property of the one – man company and the sole shareholder is cannot be separated, or the sole shareholder abuse the limited liability privilege, or something in bad faith happens, thereof disregarding the corporate personality can apply.64It is also commonly admitted that because one man company in the which the violation on of legal policies sustaining the legal entity personality is the most likely to happen ,the conation that will trigger the application of the rule piercing the corporation's veil will also apply to one –man company.[65]

D. Germany

1) Types: one man company after establishment was permitted in 1897 commercial law code: if the company had only two shareholders, and one of them refined from the company, then the company did not necessarily go dissolution. The company can continue its business.[66]One man limited company was admitted in the 1980 revised limited company act which came into force in January 1, 1981.[67] One man joint-stock company was admitted by the 1994 revised joint-stock company act.

2) Capital

A) The minimum capital requirement is DEM50,000(changed to EU 25,000 in January 1,1999).if the shareholder contribution in cash, then ¼ of the total capital should be paid in, and the shareholder should provide guarantee to the remaining part; and only up on this ,the company can apply registration. During the registration process, the court that accepted the application is entitled to examine the guarantee.

---

[63] Taylor Vs. Standard Gas & Electric Co. 35
[64] Perpper Vs Litton; Oriental Investment Co V Berclay; Joseph R. Foard Co V State Of Maryland
[65] Report S.Steven, Hand Bool On Law Of Private Corporation, Horn Book Series, West Publishing Co 96(1949) And Also See Zhao Deshu, Detail Analysis To One Man Company, China Renmin University Press,156(2004).
[66] Zhao Deshu, Detail Analysis To One Man Company, China Renmin University Press,67(2004)
[67] Limited Liability Company Can Be Incorporated By One Or Several Person In Accordance With This Law. "Limited Company Law, Article Referring Zhao Deshu, Detail Analysis To One Man Company, China Renmin University Press,72(2004)

B) This capital and guarantee requirement is also applicable to the one –man transferred from normal one (with 2 or more shareholder) if the normal one had existed less than 3 years from in corporation .if the above capital or guarantee requirements are not satisfied, then the one man company should be dissolved

3) Demonstration & Disclosure:

A) The article of association shall be notarized by the court after the shareholder signed on it

B) The amount of the capital should be specified in the article of association.

C) The company decision made by the sole shareholder should be recorded according to article 48, it m3 for the inquiry by other

D) The self-representative activities (if specified in the articles of association) should be recorded the legal document of the company (e.g. the meeting record)

E) If the one man company as described in the above 2(b) come into exist, the executive shareholder all registration in commercial register.[68]

4) Other restrictions: self- representative are generally prohibited by the law except such activities is specified in the article of association.

5) Disregard the corporate personality: the principle of disregarding corporate personality is sophisticated in Germany after the persistent development from 1920. The development in Germany may also be divided in to three stages.

A) In June 23, 1920, Germany empire court denied a company's independent personality for the fit time, saying "the sole shareholder of the company and the one –man company is independent, while when making judgment, the factors such as real life, economic demand and factual strength etc should be taken into consideration and should make different proposition according to the specific circumstances.[69] This is referred to as perspective theory (durchgrigglehre)[70]

B) In novemeber16, 1937, the Germany empire court held that when the capital of the company is in adequate, the loan made by the shareholder to the company cannot listed as prior credit right to be discharged first when the company applies bankruptcy; this judgment is based on prohibition of abuse of right prescribed in article 226 in civil law

---

[68] Ke Jv ,One Man Company ,Taiwan University Law Review, Vol. 22, 321(1993)
[69] Zhao Deshu, Detail Analysis To One Man Company, China Renmin University Press,161(2004)
[70] Id At 160

.until now; the theory in Germany for disregarding corporation personality has developed in to "abuse of right theory"

C) In may26, 1955, numberg court made a judgment71 and in 1960, the federal Supreme Court made another judgment.72Both of them indicate a new stage of the development. In 1955, Dr. Rolf Erick referred to the rule in the United States and again brought forth the "perspective theory", stating that the independence of personality. And there are two genres for the condition for disregarding- "legal theory application" and regulation application"

German court summarized the scope where the rule of disregarding corporate personality can be applied: shift off the law, violation of contractual obligation, causing damage to the third party as well as take fusion of personalities, inadequate capital and whole controlling etc which are adopted by the united state and England.

It is worth noting that: Germany, a written law country with continental legal system, relied heavily on the judgment and scholars' theory to develop the rule and conditions for disregarding corporate personality.[73]

E .France

In 1985, France promulgated the act concerning constituting one Man Company, provided a single person could constitute to e-man limited liability Company.[74]From then on one-man company comes into a new development stage.

1) Type: in France, one man limited company was recognized according to the article 34 of the court any act.[75] One –Man join-stock Company was not admitted expressly. For article 240 provides that "if the number of the share holder of the company (joint –stock-company) is less than 7 and this status last more than one year, the commercial court can dissolve the company per the application of any in rested party.[76]

2) Capital: the minimum capital requirement is FR 20,000

3) Article of association: the article association shall be made in the form of private execute certificate or notarial deed. The articles of association shall include the following item: name,

---

[71] Id At 164
[72] Id At 165 N 117
[73] Id At 168
[74] Zhao Deshu, Detailed analysis to one man company, china renmin university press 76-77(2004)
[75] "limited liability company is a company incorporate by one or more person who will assume the loss with and limited to contribute on the company" France company regulation, law press ,article 34(1999) .
[76] France company regulation ,law press ,(1999)

purpose of one Man Company, site of the Principle Company, and amount of capital and management measure.

4) Demonstration and Disclosure

 A) The name of one-man company shall include "capitalized one –man company" followed the name, at this complete name shall be record in all certificates and documents of the company.

 B) Limited liability or its initial letter "SAR L" shall be included in the company's name, and capital should be specified for single member company.[77]

5) Other restriction:

 A) Limitation on incorporation: one natural person can only incorporated one –man company and act as the sole shareholder. One limited liability company shall not be the sole shareholder of one-man company. There are also relevant procedures for related persons to supervise this[78]

 B) Limitation on the director's[79]salary: the salary of the director should be not less than 20% of the net profit and not more than 50% of net profit than gross profit. And this will come into effect after the first business year of the company.[80]

 C) Limitation on social welfare: if any director's spouse or children works together with the directive in the company, this person and the director will commonly enjoy only one person's social welfare.[81]

6) Dissolution of company: the company must be dissolved if the loss has accumulated up to 3/4the total amount of capital. There are also provisions about the liquidation of the company[82]

---

[77] France company law press ,article 34(1999)

[78] " if the company violated the above provision ,all related persons can apply to dissolve to the company. If the illegal status is caused because of the concentration of shares to one man, then no body can apply to dissolve if the concentration status last less than 1 year. Under all circumstance, the court may grant a period no more than 6 months for the company to correct the illegal status. If the illegal status has been correct when the court hear the case, the court can't make a judgment to dissolve the company." France company regulation, law press, article 36(1999)

[79] The director in one Man Company is the sole shareholder. Article 8 of provisions on the incorporation of one –man limited company ,Quoted in Zhao Deshu, , Detailed analysis to one man company, china renmin university press 330(2004)

[80] Provision on the incorporation of one man limited company ,article 10 ,Quoted in Zhao Deshu, , Detailed analysis to one man company, china renmin university press 321(2004)

[81] Provision on the incorporation of one –man limited company ,article 11 ,Quoted in Zhao Deshu, , Detailed analysis to one man company, china renmin university press 321(2004)

[82] Provision on the incorporation of one –man limited company ,article 14 ,Quoted in Zhao Deshu, , Detailed analysis to one man company, china renmin university press 321(2004)

7) Measures to protect creditors: in France, the rule of disregarding corporate personality was not adopted. They handled the dispute arising out of the abuse of corporate personality according to relevant provisions in their current legal system. For example, article 1167 of civil law provided the creditors with the right to revoke certain transactions when the company conducts fraud to the creditor or the principle company makes use of the subsidiary company to defraud the creditor. There are also provisions holding the shareholding the shareholder's personal liability to the company's debt i.e. in line with principle of piercing the corporate veil.[83]

F .India, china

Status of One person company (OPC) In Other Countries: - Various countries permit this kind of a corporate entity (China introduced one man company in October 2005) in which the promoting individual is both the director and the shareholder.[84] However, the problems with the new rules in china such as incomplete, gaps between the rules, one size fits all provision over restrictions on establishment (capital requirements, demonstration and disclosure, disregarding corporate personality) and problem of the scheme as well.[85] That why the writer shall prefer the other countries experiences, predominately India draft bill of OPC, than china one Man Company.

The amended company law of Pakistan permits one person to form a single-member company by filing with registrar, at the time of incorporation, a nomination in the prescribed form indicating at least two individuals to act as nominee director and alternate nominee director. These are one possible provision on Ethiopian one man company law to draft in the future.

In US, several states permit the formation and operation of a single-member Limited Liability Company (LLC).even in USA one man company was the recent development the US legal systems. Hence, there was a problem at operation stage of one Man Company in several states. In China, one person is allowed to apply for opening a limited company with a minimum capital of 1, 00,000 Yuan[86] where as in Ethiopia 250,000 birr in accordance with the recommendation of the writer of the mini paper. The amended law of China prescribes that the owner should pay the investment capital at one time and bars him from opening a second

---

[83] Zhao Deshu, , Detailed analysis to one man company, china renmin university press 195-196(2004)
[84] KA JV, one man company, Taiwan university law review, 1993, vol. 22, s2.
[85] Wan tianhong ,comparative study on one man company , law press,(2003) and see also Lin Guoguan ,one man company, yudan law magazine,1997,vol.22.
[86] Wang Yong, introduction to one man company, available at , http://www.ccelaws.com/int/art page/3/art-2620. also see Yang Beijing, brief introduction to the one man company rule available at: http://lawi.china lawinfo.com/nWlaw2002/SLC.asp?Db=art&Gid=335579286.(Date of accessed may 30-2013.)

company of the same kind.[87] The same concept should be incorporation into Ethiopian to draft law of one Man Company in near future.

In most countries, the law governing companies enables a single-member company to have more than one director and grants exemptions to such companies from holding AGMs, though records and documents are to be maintained.[88]

Further, aspects relating to nomination in case of death of sole member and change of status of the firm are also covered. So that the death of single member does not affect the legal personality of one Man Company due to this the existence the company will continues business activities.[89]

4.2 The possible lesson for Ethiopia to incorporate one man company in to our legal system

The proposed introduction of one-person company into the legal system is a move that would encourage corporatization of business and entrepreneurship. At present, an entrepreneur in Ethiopia has to find another person to implement his skills through incorporation of one Man Company while in the EU,US, UK, Australia, Germany, Singapore, Pakistan, etc; a single person can company. Since OPC is only one shareholder corporate entity, where legal and financial liability is limited to the company asset only[90],However, to prevent the sole shareholder of a one-person limited company from taking advantage of the company's assets for his/her use, the revised Company Law imposes more stringent requirements on a one-person company than it does on companies with multiple shareholders, including i) raising the minimum registered capital to 250,000 EB which must be fully contributed in a lump sum when the company is established, ii) specifying the nature of the one-shareholder company (either one natural person or one legal person) on its business license, iii) stipulating that a natural person/physical person may only set up a single one-person company, and such one person company may not set up another one-person company (although note that no similar restriction has been imposed on a one person company established by a legal person/juridical person such as another corporation), iv) requiring important decisions (such as decisions on

---

[87] Infra note 81
[88] .Note, one man corporation –scope and limitation, 100 U pa L.Rev.853,1951-1952. Also see Wang Yong, introduction to one man company, available at http://www.ccelaws.com/int/art page/3/art-2620. (Date of accessed at jun4 -2013).
[89] One Person Company Concept In Indian Company Law :The Draft Companies Bill, 2(2009)
[90] Ibid

amendments to the articles of association, company's operational guidelines and investment plans)made by the shareholder to be in writing and the company to keep a file of such documents upon their signing by the shareholder, v) requiring the financial reports of a one person company for each fiscal year of Ethiopia(July1-June 30) to be inspected and audited by an accounting firm, and vi) providing that a shareholder of a one person company may be jointly and severally liable for the debts of the company if he/she fails to prove that his/her assets are independent from the assets of the one man company(piercing corporate veil).[91]

Permitting and regulating one-person companies is conducive to encouraging investment generally and will give more flexibility to large company groups (particularly foreign enterprises which have group operations in the PRC) to manage the overall group corporate structure. Considering the higher risks that the shareholders of a one-person company might face, it is likely to be the case that one person companies are not as popular among natural persons as they are in large corporate group structures.

4.3 Possible draft of one Man Company

For Ethiopia, writer of this paper recommends the main articles as guild line elements for one Man Company in summery form.

1) Type: a nature person or legal entity can establish a one –man limited liability Company in Ethiopian territory.

2) Capital: the minimum amount of registered capital of one –Man Company shall be 250,000EB and all the capital specified in article of association shall be full paid in capital.[92]

3) Demonstration and Disclosure: a one limited liability company shall, in the company registration, give clear indication that it is solely-found by one nature person or legal entity and the same shall be specified in the business license of the company.

4) Other limitations

---

[91] Pinsent Masons, Supra note 35.
[92] Company law of people of china 59 ff fixing the capital but US law" more flexible" on minimum capital fixation rather it shall be determined case by case base .but all other countries fix the capital for their one man company. so, Ethiopia should learn from anther countries experiences to fix the capital of one man company by taken to the economic reality of the country and the current value of money when the legislator fix the capital of the one man company.

A) One natural person is allowed to establish merely one –person limited liability Company. So, natural person shall not establish parallel one Man Company or more than one company rather only one man company allows for physical person, whereas legal person can establish double one-man company in Ethiopian territory and out of Ethiopia.

B) Article of association: the article of association of a one person limited liability company shall be formulated by the shareholder.

C) Resolution of the company: a one- man company has board of directors and the chair man of board of director the owner of the one man company. when the shareholder make a decision on any the matters as listed in commercial cod of Ethiopia, he shall make it in written form sign and preserve the same in the company. However, in the environmental and human right issues the chair man together with other out sider, director, shall pass the decision through majority vote.

D) Financial report and audit: a one person limited liability company shall make a financial report by the end of every fiscal year, "(ymajemeraw hamila1- ymiyibqawe sene30)", which shall be audited by an accounting firm.

5) Disregard corporate personality:

If the share holder of a one man company is unable to prove that the property of one man company is independent from his owner property, he shall be joint liability for the debts of the company

A) The shareholder should not injure any of the interests of the company or of other shareholder by busing the shareholder's right, or injury the interests of any creditor of the company by abusing the privilege of limited liability. Where any of the shareholders of the company evades its debts by abusing the privilege of limited liability, and the creditor was suffered significant damage, it shall be severally and jointly liable for the debts of the company.[93]

B) Moreover, with respected to good corporate governance, the future draft should take into account of the seven characteristics of it. Such as discipline, transparency, independence, accountability, responsibility, fairness, and social responsibility[94] but the

---

[93] Company law of people's republic of china, article 20, article 58-64(NB. the writer take the concept from this provision by modifying and changing some provision since there were a problems in china one man company for instances no board of director for one man company, no provision about the social responsibility of one man company and its owner of the company).

[94] JOHON L.COLLEY,JR.JACQUELINE L.DOYLE GEORGE W .LOGAN WALLACE STETTINUS,WHAT IS CORPORATE GOVERNANCE?,TATA MCGRAW-HILL PUBLISHING COMPANY LIMITED, INC.NEW YORK(2005)

composition of board[95] of directors should includes single member and the out sider of the company for the sack of social responsibility; the size BOD[96] should be a few and it has to be odd in number since it is important to pass a decision of the environmental and labor right issue in connection with one man company. But no board of director in china one man company but one director allows in Indian bill on one Man Company[97] and their rule is silent about social responsibility of the one man company as per the principle of good corporate governance. Therefore, Ethiopia should learn from china and India to draft law on the board of directors even from out side of a single member company to protect the environmental and HR issues.

In addition to this, rule should be made clear that every one man company shall have an auditor. Single Member Company enjoys limited liability and creditors can rely on the capital. Creditors or third parties could not know the financial position of the one man company unless investigation is carried out at a certain interval by an independent professional auditor. The writer of this paper, therefore, strongly recommends that every one man company be required to have auditors as one of its organs.

A .The legal scheme provided by scholar

Professor Rotondi in his limited liability of the individual trader: one Man Company or commercial foundation (1973-1974) provided the basic criteria needed to be established for one Man Company as fallows[98] these could be guild line elements for the introduction of one Man Company in Ethiopia

1) The right to establish such an entity should be available to anyone with the capacity, whether a natural or legal person.

2) Capital: a substantial minimum capital, fully paid, at a level certainly not lower that for joint-stock company where such levels are fixed:

---

[95] COMMISSION OF THE EROPEAN COMMUNTIES,BRUSSELS21.5.2003,COM (2003) 284 FINAL, COMMUNICATION FROM THE COMMISSION TO THE COUNCIL AND THE EUROPEAN PARLIAMENT, modernizing company law and enhancing corporate governance in the European union-plan to move forward at 15ff(2003)
[96] Id at 21
[97] How many Directors in a OPC? India Section 149 (1) says, Every company shall have a Board of Directors consisting of individuals as directors and shall have—(a) a minimum number of three directors in the case of a public company, two directors in the case of a private company, and one director in the case of a One Person Company. Available at http://www.mca.gov.in/Ministry/pdf/The_Companies_Bill_2012.pdf
[98] Mario Rotondi, limited liability of the individual trader: one Man Company or commercial foundation, 48TU.L.Rev. 1973-1974,(999-1009),p1007.

3) Demonstration & disclosure:

   A) Mandatory provisions for the formal execution of the memorandum of association, designating to the objective ,the denomination (defining in the name the nature of the body),the capital ,the location of the administrative offices, and the term of existence of the body should be established;

   B) A system of public registration of the memorandum and article of association should be established along with notice in the appropriate legal commercial Gazettes (with the same formalities for any later amendment to constitution i.e. article or memorandum of association.

   C) The annual account, to be subject of official audit, should be published

4) Liquidation:[99]

   A) Provision for liquidation in the of a loss, which is not made up, of the major part of the asset

   B) Provision for voluntary liquidation, with appropriate guarantees and publicity for the benefit of creditor

5) Liabilities:[100]

   A) Any appropriation of assets from the business other than cash dividend on trading profit should be prohibited

   B) Manager should be personally liable
      i. If they are in the breach of the fundamental regulations
      ii. If they infringe guarantees for third parties,
      iii. If they act ultra virus the constitution (lack due care and due diligence)
      iv. If they continue the business after due notice for dissolution or
      v. If they finalize a liquidation knowing that there are liabilities still outstanding

   C) Security should be given for valuation of the assets original contributed to the company, with personal liability on the part of the promoter in case of fraud (with similar security and liability for further accretions to the corporate assets)

---

[99] Professor Rotondi in his limited liability of the individual trader: one man company or commercial foundation?(1973-1974) and also see Cui Zaifei, a comparative analysis of one man company, (date accessed 12-13-2012 17:06:45)
[100] Ibid

Rights and duties of single member

Rights: When once a person becomes a single member of one man Company he or she is entitled to exercise all the rights of single member until he/she ceases to be a member in accordance with the provisions of the draft regulation of one man company or statues of the one man company. Such rights cannot be taken away from single member unless he give his consent. Some of these rights can be exercised by single member individually and others along with one man company itself. Rights of single member of one Man Company can take all net profit in principle. But some time, some amount of net profit given to the founder (if there is founder), manger(s), and some amount reserved for the one man company itself.

Individual rights (owner): Include single member rights to[101]

- Participate in annual net profit
- Share in the net proceeds on a winding –up ,on surpluses asset
- Transfer one man company itself subject to any restriction
- Inspect the registers, indexes, returns and copies of ownership certificate one man company etc. Kept by the one man company and obtain extracts or copy thereof
- Obtain copies or of memorandum and articles on request and payment of the prescribed fee.
- Receive a copy or original of statutory report
- Remove directors
- Obtain a copy of the profit and loss account and the balance sheet with the auditor's report receive a money in the capital of company and the surplus assets, if any, on the one man company's liquidation
- Directors and officers through specific limitations on authority

Public and Owner Access to Company Information

The one man Company Law takes an entirely different, much more public, approach. The one man Company Law provides that the public has the right to access basic company registration information and further provides that the registration authority must provide consulting assistance in accessing that information. The public will now have access to the following information on limited liability one man companies:[102]

---

[101] Warner Fuller, the incorporated individual: A study of the one man company ,51 Harv.L.Rev.1373(1937-1938)
[102] BERNARD F.CATALDO, Supra note 24 at 475ff

- Name
- registered address
- Legal representative
- registered capital
- Business type
- Scope of business
- Termination date
- Identity of shareholder

Under our system, all of this information is considered essential for creditor protection. The one man Company Law takes the reasonable position that creditor protection requires this basic information be freely available to the public. Since the identity of shareholder is freely available, it is now impossible to use a Chinese limited liability company to conceal the identity of the true party in interest. Therefore, Ethiopia should take these kind experiences from china.

Abuse of single Shareholder Rights and Piercing the Corporate Veil

The single shareholder company section, which provides the shareholder of a single shareholder company who cannot prove that the finances of the company are independent of his or her own finances, will have joint liability for the debts of the company. This "piercing the corporate veil" concept is entirely new to Ethiopia and though it may be useful to prevent obvious abuses, it could also be used to undermine the concept of limitation of liability, which is the foundation of the corporation law concept in one Man Company.[103]

Limitations on Third Party Loans and Guarantees

The possible rules of the one man Company Law seeks to remedy this in the future. The possible Article provides that one man company may invest in another company, but prohibits it from doing so in a manner that it becomes jointly liable for the debts of the other company. Other Article provides additional rules concerning the providing of investment or debt guarantees to third party companies:[104]

---

[103] Supra note 7o at 5ff.
[104] Id

- The investment or guarantee must be approved by either the board of directors or by the shareholders, as provided in the articles of association
- Where the articles of association limit the amount of investment or guarantee, such limit may not be exceeded
- The shareholder must approve a guarantee provided to a shareholder or to the person actually controlling the company. In such cases, the benefiting shareholder may not participate in the decision and approval must be by a majority of the remaining shareholder.

Under this approach, the senior management of the company and individual directors has no authority to make investments or to provide guarantees by any means. This is a significant departure from future practice of Ethiopia

Legal Remedies for Improper Acts of Directors and Senior Management

The one man company seeks to address this matter directly. First, the regulation should expressly prohibit directors and senior management from engaging in the following acts:[105]

1) Misappropriating company funds;

2) Depositing company funds into an individual account;

3) Loaning company funds or providing a company guaranty without owner of one man company approval;

4) Signing a contract or trading with another company in violation of the articles of association, unless the owner or single member expressly consents;

5) Without shareholder/owner of the company consent, seeking business opportunities for oneself or for any other person by taking advantage of one's authority, or operating for oneself or for any other person any business similar to that of the company for which one works, without shareholder/single member consent; (6) Taking commissions on a company transaction ;

7) Disclosing company secrets without permission;

8) Other acts inconsistent with the obligation of fidelity to the one man company.

---

[105] Steven M, Supra note 22 at 6

B. New Draft Bill For Ethiopia from other countries

According to 347 of OHADA, Where the company is a sole proprietorship, the provisions of Articles 558 to 561 of the Uniform Act, excluding those of the second paragraphs of Articles 558 and 559 below, shall apply. The provisions of this Chapter which are not repugnant hereto shall also apply.[106] The writer directly quoted the provision since it could be relevance to draft one man company in Ethiopia with respect to the any decision therein.

Chapter 5, special case of a public limited company with a single shareholder[107]

Article 558

Where a public limited company has only one shareholder, the decisions to be taken at a meeting, be they decisions falling within the jurisdiction of the extraordinary general meeting or those falling within the jurisdiction of the ordinary general meeting, shall be taken by that shareholder.

The provisions of Articles 516 to 577 of this Uniform Act that are not contrary to the provisions of this article shall apply.

Article 559

The single shareholder shall, within a period of six months following the close of the fiscal year, take all the decisions falling within the jurisdiction of the annual ordinary general meeting.

The decisions shall be taken upon the reports of the managing director and of the auditor who attend general meetings in accordance with the provisions of Article 721 of this Uniform Act.

Article 560

Decisions taken by the single shareholder shall be in the form of minutes which shall be filed in the records of the company.

Article 561

All decisions taken by the single shareholder who would have been published in a newspaper carrying legal notices if they had been taken by a general meeting shall be published in the same manner

---

[106] UNIFORM ACT RELATING TO COMMERCIAL COMPANIES AND ECONOMIC INTEREST GROUP Translation The Council of Ministers of the Organization for the Harmonization of Business Law in Africa (OHADA), article 347.
[107] Ibid ,chapter 5 OHADA,(article 558-562)

Therefore, chapter five of OHADA provisions (558-561) could be guiding element to draft one man company in Ethiopia with respect to any decision thereof so that it would be part of the possible draft of one Man Company in Ethiopia.

Following are some of the glimpses of the provisions in the new Draft Bill. The provisions are those which deal with aspect of One Person Company.[108] This will be very much relevant to draft on one Man Company in Ethiopia. (See the detail as follow) One Person Company is defined as: "One Person Company" means a company which has only one person as a member" Chapter II deals with the Incorporation of the Companies. Section 3(1) (c) deals with the formation of One Person Company. It states: [109] "One person, where the company to be formed is to be a One Person Company, by subscribing their names or his name to a memorandum in the manner prescribed and complying with the requirements of this Act in respect of registration:

Provided that the memorandum of a One Person Company shall indicate the name of the person who shall, in the event of the subscriber's death, disability or otherwise, become the member of the company.

Provided further that it shall be the duty of the member of a One Person Company to intimate the Registrar the change, if any, in the name of the person referred to in the preceding proviso and indicated in the memorandum within such time and in such form as may be prescribed, and any such change shall not be deemed to be an alteration of the memorandum"[110]

Section 5(1) deals with the memorandum of the One Person Company. It states "The memorandum of a company shall state— the last letters and word "OPC Limited" in the case of a One Person limited company"[111].

Section 13(1) a, b, c deals with alteration of articles including the conversion of Private Companies, Public Companies to One Person Companies and vice-versa. One very important feature of the OPC concept is the conduction of Annual General Meeting.[112]

Section 85(1) of the Draft Bill excludes One Person Company from holding Annual General Meeting at least once in a year.[113]

---

[108] NB writer take only important provisions from India draft law and other countries law on one man company by making contextualizing into Ethiopia legal systems and its people
[109] Indian draft bill on one person company(OPC) section 3(1)
[110] Supra note 84 and 86.
[111] Supra note 35 as section 5(1)
[112] Adikool, One Person Company Concept ,one-person-company-concept-103-1.html
(Published: June 4, 2013, 3:34 pm) at 4 (2006)

Section 171 is perhaps the most important and fascinating provision to look out for. It states:"Contracts by One Person Companies. 171. (1) Where a One Person Company limited by shares or by guarantee enters into a contract with the sole member of the company who is also director of the company, the company shall, unless the contract is in writing, ensure that the terms of the contract or offer are contained in a memorandum or are recorded in the minutes of the first meeting of the Board of Directors of the company held next after the entering into the contract Provided that nothing in this sub-section shall apply to contracts entered into by the company in the ordinary course of its business.[114]

2) The company shall inform the Registrar about every contract entered into by the company and recorded in the minutes of the meeting of its Board of Directors under sub-section (1) within fifteen days of the date of approval by the Board of Directors with such fee as may be prescribed, or with such additional fee as may be prescribed within the time specified, under section 364.So, Ethiopia should take this procedure from India to draft one man company in the area of board of directors' ,however, in china no rule for board of director for single member company.

3) Where the company fails to inform the Registrar under sub-section (2) before the expiry of the period specified under section 364 with additional fee, the company shall be punishable with fine which shall not be less than twenty-five thousand birr but which may extend to one 50,000 birr and every officer who is in default shall be punishable with imprisonment for a term which may extend to six months or with fine which shall not be less than twenty-five thousand rupees but which may extend to one 50,000 birr, or with both."[115]

Therefore, these could be main guiding elements and the possible draft for one man company in Ethiopia in near future since the writer specify 25 basic rule above for one man company and international experiences therein which is very much relevant to draft one man company as building block in the content of regulation for the future research on these area.

---

[113] Ibid

[114] Indian draft bill, section 171(1) which relevant for Ethiopia future draft on one Man Company available at http://www.mca.gov.in/Ministry/pdf/The_Companies_Bill_2012.pdf

[115] NB writer take only important provisions from India draft law and other countries law on one Man Company by making contextualizing into Ethiopia legal systems and its people.

5 Recommendation and conclusion

5.1 Conclusion

The writer can draw a conclusion from the above analysis that possible draft provision related to one man company in the draft of one man company law are incomplete and too simple generally; examining the specific draft provisions form other countries experiences, there exist not a few problems.

Therefore, the possible draft provisions and basic rule still need to be consummated and perfected. This is a field very difficult to clear the line are difficult to draw, and it is a challenge to the legislator in the future. The analyses made in this article through comparing with relevant provision in other countries like EU, US, UK, Germany, Francis, and India raise some question need to be dealt with.

For the future, the legislator and justice system of Ethiopia may need more effort to draft one man company by specify the detailed and operational standards guild line for the investors protection and the market development in business activities. The legislature should try their best on the design and introduce the rule one man company to give enough incentive to the investors and better grantee the third party (particularly creditors) to adopt formal one –Man Company. Instead of defacto one man company (PLC in effect or in practice of PLC in Ethiopia which the most problematic company), meanwhile encourage creditors to supervise the one man company and its single shareholder.

The executive branch should improve their process technology, to be more active and effective regulating one man companies. All entities in the market, together with legislative, judicial and administrative should commonly make more effort to keep the market developing smoothly and quickly.

Finally, the paper contain the possible draft one man company in Ethiopia and the possible leason from the international experiences on single member company and its basic rules as guild line elements for the introduction of one man company into Ethiopian legal system after the factual analysis of the country and the global forced condition for Ethiopia.

5.2 Recommendation

Before introduce one man company in to Ethiopia legal system, there should be have adequate regulation to govern every matters like founder, capital and contribution in kind, public registration, management, good corporate governance (BOD, Mangers, auditors, transparency), creditor(s), heirs and the like.

Well- studied before incorporation and well prepared regulation on one man company in context of Ethiopia current circumstances so that properly implementation of regulation of one man company with improved intuitional capacity building since the institution is vital in super visional activities over one man company in Ethiopia in order to avoid the abuse act of the company.

Therefore, Introduction of one company in to Ethiopia legal system should need appropriate regulation and proper implementation of law. So that one man company should be need of technocrat managers from the market; and selection of them at base of market based competition in order to take the best of them.

The chair man of the board of director could be the owner of one Man Company but with respect to the member of board of director from out side single member company should be recommended for the seek of social responsibility as good corporate governance since a well-managed one man company will be aware of, and respond to, social issue, placing a high priority on ethical standards. The good corporate citizen should be increasingly seen as one that is non-discriminatory, non-exploitative, and responsive with regard to environmental and human rights (e.g. labor right within one Man Company) issues. One man company should likely to experience indirect economic benefit such as improved productivity and corporate reputation by taking those factors into consideration.

The single member can be manger of one Man Company as member manger; he has two capacities as an agent and the owner of the one man company. hence, as agent all his act in due care and due diligence expected from him as "bonus pater familias" (good father of family), however, if he involve in management of one man company without the due care and due diligence, then he loss his advantage of limited corporate liability because as agent of the company, he shall be liable personally beyond the asset of the one man company.

With regard to employed manger or non-member mangers liability as agent based on lack of due care and due diligence but at time of rendering decision by court against employed manager should taken into account of the personal circumstances of employed manger(s) of one man company. Therefore, before pass the judgment on the liability of employed manager, the judges should have known the less economic capacity of him to discharge the decision of the court.

On other hand , to implement properly and effectively one man company in Ethiopia ,a country should over come the short coming on the general competition law(such as the definition of market share, non-regulation of anti-competitive marger, non-determination of choice between the per se and rule-of- reason approach and non-pro activeness of enforcement). Therefore, improvement and implementation in competition law minimize the market dominance of one man company and anti- competitive marger of Man Company with other one man company, share company, and PLC. These margers affect the interest of third party (like creditors).

With respect to the third party (creditors) interest should be protected before, during winding –up the one man company or owner of company passed away then their conflict of interest arise between heirs and creditors. Even if the death single member does not affected legal personality of one Man Company and also his death does not affect the interest of creditors since priority should be given to the creditors at any time. But at time of wind up of one Man Company the secured creditors should have priority over unsecured creditors.

General in the future, defacto one man company should not benefit from its wrongful acts by raising defense in court room(like no legal personality, no registration ,as preliminary objection should not be acceptable defenses because defacto one man company should not benefit from his/her wrongful acts) if there were litigation with other companies.

References

Books

1. RECOMMENDATIONS AND POSITION PAPER OF THE BUSINESS COMMUNITY ON THE REVIS OF THE COMMERCIAL CODE OF ETHIOPIA Prepared by A TEAM OF FOURTEEN NATIONAL EXPER 34 (july2008) BY ETHIOPIAN CHAMBER OF COMMERCE

2. BERNARD F.CATALDO,LIMITED LIABILITY WITH ONE MAN COMPANIES AND SUBSIDIARY CORPORTION:18 LAW AND CONTEPT PROBS 474(1953

3. AVTAR SINGH, COMPANY LAW, FOURTEENTH EDITION, 533FF(2004)

Article and journal

1. Beihui Miao, A Comparative Study of Legal Framework for Single Member Company in European Union and China 1 School of Law, King's College London, University of London, London, United Kingdom Correspondence,WC2R 2LS, England, United Kingdom. (Tel: 44-788-851-5557. E-mail:beihui.miao@kcl.ac.uk),

2. Beihui Miao, A Comparative Study of Legal Framework for Single Member Company in European Union and China, at 7

3. Steven M. Dickinson, Harris & Moure, Introduction to the New Company Law of the People's Republic of China, at 3

4. Mario Rotondi, limited liability of the individual trade: one –man company or commercial foundation:48 TULL.L.Rev.474,(1973-1974)

5. Warner Fuller, the incorporated individual: A study of the one man company, 51 Harv.L.Rev.1373 (1937-1938)

6. KA JV, one man company, Taiwan university law review, vol.22,s2. (1993)

7. Wan tianhong ,comparative study on one man company , law press,(2003) and see also Lin Guoguan ,one man company, yudan law magazine, ,vol.22. (1997)

8. Hong Deqin , European Union: Theory And Policy, Graduate School Of Europe And The United States Of Central Academe At 4. German Stock Act ,China Political And Law University ,(2002)

9. Jan Yuan Ju Zhi, One Man Company, Dongbei University, Jurisprudence, Volume 37, No 1, 39 (1973),

10. Limited Liability Company Can Be Incorporated By One Or Several Person In Accordance With This Law. "Limited Company Law, Article Referring Zhao Deshu, Detail Analysis To One Man Company, China Renmin University Press,72(2004)

11. Report S.Steven, Hand Bool On Law Of Private Corporation, Horn Book Series, West Publishing Co 96(1949)

Laws

1. Federal Democratic Republic Of Ethiopia Constitution of 1995, Article 41(1) Article 40(1)

2. Commercial cod of Ethiopia in 1960's (article 211, 308,309, 339,531(2), comm.cod)

3. Civil Cod Of Ethiopia Article (1675cc, 2188,2189 Cc. article 2187 and article 2188cc) 4.Competition proclamation of Ethiopia

4. Insurances proclamation ion Ethiopia proclamation no 746/2012 (insurances share company).

5. bank proclamation of Ethiopia, proclamation no 592/2008(allows only bank share company)

6. One Person Company Concept in Indian Company Law : The Draft Companies Bill, 2(2009) available at http://www.mca.gov.in/Ministry/pdf/The_Companies_Bill_2012.pdf

7. Law related to natural person and company(Gesetzuber das personon und Gesellschaftserercht), Item 638 & 641

8. Twelfth Council Company Law Directive, Article 2 , & Article 3-5

9. France company law press ,article 34 &36(1999)

Website

1. Can One Person form a Company? Available at www.companiesnow.com.au, date of accessed may 30-2013

2. Wang Yong, introduction to one man company, available at http://www.ccelaws.com/int/art page/3/art-2620.(Date accessed may24-2013)

3. Yang Beijing, brief introduction to the one man company rule available at: http://lawi.china lawinfo.com/nWlaw2002/SLC.asp?Db=art&Gid=335579286.(Date of accessed may 30-2013.)

4. Note, one man corporation –scope and limitation, 100 U pa L.Rev.853,1951-1952. Also see Wang Yong, introduction to one man company, available at, http://www.ccelaws.com/int/art page/3/art-2620. (Date of accessed at jun4 -2013).

Cases

1. Arnold V Phillips, 313 U.S.583;61 S.Ct. 1102,(1941).In Which An Entrepreneur Who Wanted To Operate A Brewery Invested Authored Share Capital $50,000in Cash And Another 75,000 As The Loan To The Corporation For Its Operation, Upon The Insolvency Of The Corporation, It 75,000was Treated As A Capital Contribution. Bernard F. Cataldo, Limited Liability With One Man Companies And Subsidiary Corporation,18 Aw &Contemp.Probs.474,484-485(1953)

2. The Development Of The Rule In The United States Is Referring To Relative Part Of Zhao Deshu, Detail Analysis To One Man Company, China Renmin University Press,39(2004).

3. People V The Northern River Sugar Refining Co ; State V Standard Oil Co. Moore & Handle Hardware Co. V Towers Hardware Co. ;Hahine V California Petroleum & Asphalt Co.

4. Berry V Old South Engraving Co.(1993)34

5. Taylor Ve. Standard Gas & Electric Co. 35

6. Perpper V Litton; Oriental Investment Co V Berclay; Joseph R. Foard Co V State Of Maryland